THE
CREATION STORY

Retold by Mary Packard
Illustrated by Joe Veno

A Golden Book • New York
Golden Books Publishing Company, Inc., Racine, Wisconsin 53404

Once the world was dark and still—
Just empty space for God to fill.

Then God made the heavens bright!
With one command, he created light.

He shaped the earth—land high and low—

And covered it with things that grow.

The oceans he made deep and blue.

He made the lakes and rivers, too.

To light the day, God made the sun—

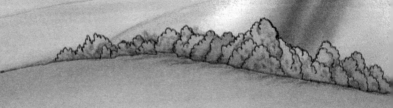

And added rainbows just for fun!

He hung the moon so round and bright,
And twinkling stars to shine at night.

God brought life to the ocean floor,

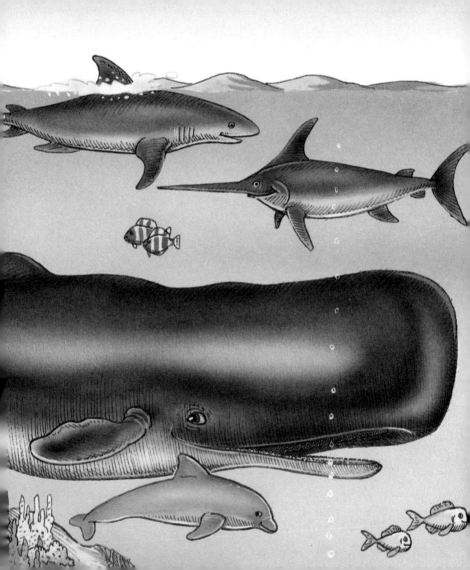

Then filled the sky with birds that soar.

On land he sent beasts great and small

And man and woman to watch over all.

Our earth, its gifts, the sky above,

God made all these to show his love.